VideoWorkshop

for

Special Education
Student Learning Guide with CD-ROM

Diana Murphy

Rebecca Evers
Winthrop University

Boston   New York   San Francisco
Mexico City   Montreal   Toronto   London   Madrid   Munich   Paris
Hong Kong   Singapore   Tokyo   Cape Town   Sydney

Copyright © 2003 Pearson Education, Inc.

All rights reserved. No part of the material protected by this copyright notice may be reproduced or utilized in any form or by any means, electronic or mechanical, including photocopying, recording, or by any information storage and retrieval system, without written permission from the copyright owner.

To obtain permission(s) to use material from this work, please submit a written request to Allyn and Bacon, Permissions Department, 75 Arlington Street, Boston, MA 02116 or fax your request to 617-848-7320.

ISBN   0-205-37795-5

Printed in the United States of America

11 12 13 14 15 16 17   08 07 06 05 04

Student Learning Guide to *Video Workshop for Special Education* p. 1

Preface

This Student Learning Guide accompanies the *Allyn & Bacon Video Workshop for Special Education*. It is designed to enhance your experience with the videos.

Features:

- **Learning Objectives** focus your learning.
- **Observation Questions** focus on the video itself.
- **Next Step** asks you to go beyond the video by answering questions or completing projects.
- **Connecting to the Web** provides relevant websites for further study.

Student Learning Guide to *Video Workshop for Special Education*

Use this grid to correlate the modules in *Video Workshop for Special Education* to your Allyn & Bacon textbook.

	Hardman, Drew and Egan *Human Exceptionality*, 7/e	Hallahan and Kauffmann *Exceptional Learners*, 9/e	Vaughn, Bos, and Schumm *Teaching Exceptional, Diverse and At-Risk Students*, 3/e	Friend and Bursuck *Including Students with Special Needs*, 3/e	Peterson and Hittie *Inclusive Teaching: Creating Effective Schools for All Learners*	Smith *Introduction to Special Education*, 5/e	Smith et al, *Teaching Students with Special Needs in Exclusive Settings*, 4/e
1: The Individualized Education Plan	Ch. 1	Ch. 1	Ch. 1, 2	Ch. 2	Ch. 4	Ch. 2	Ch. 4
2: Inclusion, Collaboration, and the Least Restrictive Environment	Ch. 1	Ch. 1, 2	Ch. 1	Ch. 1, 3	Ch. 1, 4, 5	Throughout	Ch. 1, 2
3: Cultural and Linguistic Diversity	Ch. 1	Ch. 3	Ch. 10, 11	Ch. 7	Ch. 7	Ch. 3	Ch. 13, throughout
4: Learning Disabilities and Attention Deficit Hyperactivity Disorder	Ch. 6, 7	Ch. 5, 6	Ch. 5	Ch. 6, 7	Ch. 7	Ch. 4	Ch. 5, 6
5: Mental Retardation	Ch. 9	Ch. 4	Ch. 8	Ch. 5	Ch. 7	Ch. 6	Ch. 8
6: Communication, Language and Speech Impairments	Ch. 10	Ch. 8	Ch. 6	Ch. 6	Ch. 13	Ch. 5	Ch. 11
7: Visual and Hearing Impairments	Ch. 14, 15	Ch. 9, 10	Ch. 9	Ch. 5	Ch. 13	Ch. 10, 11	Ch. 9
8: Emotional and Behavioral Disorders	Ch. 8	Ch. 7	Ch. 7	Ch. 6	Ch. 10	Ch. 8	Ch. 7
9: Traumatic Brain Injury and Physical Disabilities	Ch. 11, 12, 13, 16	Ch. 11	Ch. 9	Ch. 5	Ch. 7	Ch. 9, 13	Ch. 10
10: Working with Parents and Families	Ch. 1	Ch. 13	Ch. 4		Ch. 2, 3, 11		Ch. 3

Table of Contents

Module 1: Special Education Process: Individualized Education Plans 5
Video Clip 1: Individualized Education Plan

Module 2: Inclusion, Collaboration, and Least Restrictive Environment 11
Video Clip 2: Inclusion
Video Clip 3: The Collaborative Process

Module 3: Cultural and Linguistic Diversity and Students at Risk 19
Video Clip 4: Teaching in Bilingual Classrooms

Module 4: Learning Disabilities and Attention Deficit Hyperactivity Disorder 25
Video Clip 5: ADHD
Video Clip 6: Learning Disabilities

Module 5: Mental Retardation 35
Video Clip 7: Mental Retardation

Module 6: Communication Disorders, Language and Speech Impairments 41
Video Clip 1: Individualized Education Plan

Module 7: Sensory Disorders: Visual and Hearing Impairments 47
Video Clip 8: Visual Impairment
Video Clip 9: Hearing Impairment

Module 8. Emotional and Behavioral Disorders 57
Video Clip 10: Behavior Disorders

Module 9. Traumatic Brain Injury and Physical Disabilities 63
Video Clip 11: Traumatic Brain Injury
Video Clip 12: Physical Disabilities

Module 10. Working with Parents and Families 71
Video Clip 13: Working with Parents and Families

Module 1: Special Education Process: The Individualized Education Plan

Learning Objectives:

After completing this module, you will be able to
- Describe the process required to develop an IEP.
- Name and define the required components of the IEP.
- List the IEP team members required by I.D.E.A.-97.
- Summarize the roles/responsibilities of individual team members.
- Review family rights, including the Due Process Procedures.
- Discuss how to help parents understand the IEP process.

Video Clip 1: Individualized Education Plan

Observation Questions:

1. What is the purpose of an IEP?

   _____

   _____

   _____

   _____

2. What role does the family play in the IEP process?

   _____

   _____

   _____

   _____

Student Learning Guide to *Video Workshop for Special Education*

3. Why does Douglas need an IEP? What factors should be considered when deciding that Douglas needs an IEP?

Next Step:

1. Based on what you know about Douglas's deficits, what would be your recommendation for placement?
    - What else do you need to know to determine the best placement? Use your textbook to determine what else might be included in this IEP session.

p. 7　　Student Learning Guide to *Video Workshop for Special Education*

2. Explain the origin of the Individual Education Plan.
   - How did educators plan for special needs students before IEPs?

_____

_____

_____

_____

_____

_____

_____

3. A male student in your fourth period class has been acting the class clown and failing to complete his schoolwork. His mother is concerned and believes that he should receive special education services. While you have some concerns you do not believe he need special education services. What strategies, resources, and support services could help you in addressing the situation?

_____

_____

_____

_____

_____

_____

_____

4. Form a small group with two/three members of your class. Then using the websites listed in *Connecting to the Web* as resources, the group should construct a handbook telling about the IEP process. Your target audience is the family of students with special needs. Provide tips for family participation in the special education process, information about family rights and responsibilities, explain possible attendees at IEP meetings, and summarize the roles/responsibilities of special education individual team members. Include any other information you think a family may want to know. You can use either a word processing or publishing program to develop the handbook. Use the space below to brainstorm your ideas.

MODULE ONE Connecting to the Web:

The National Information Center for Children and Youth with Disabilities. This page follows a student through the process of evaluation and IEP development. http://nichcy.org/pubs/basicpar/bpltext.htm

Federal Resource Center for Special Education. The FRC supports a nationwide technical assistance network to respond to the needs of students with disabilities, especially students from under-represented populations, follow the link to Technical Assistance. http://www.dssc.org/frc

Wrightslaw is the website of Pete Wright, an attorney whose practice is devoted to helping children with special education needs. Follow this link to information about IEPs. http://www.wrightslaw.com/advoc/articles/iep_guidance.html

The Walter Reed Army Medical Center. The Army Medical Center has a handbook for parents. This link leads to Chapter Four: Parent Role in the Educational Process.
http://www.wramc.amedd.army.mil/departments/pediatrics/efmp/handbook/CH4.htm

LDOnline provides informative articles plus useful forms to help parents and educators make the most of the I.E.P. process.
http://www.ldonline.org/ld_indepth/iep/iep.html

Individualized Education Programs – NICHCY Briefing Paper
http://www.nichcy.org/pubs/otherpub/lg2txt.htm
This publication provides substantial guidance regarding the legal requirements for developing a student's IEP. It is a verbatim reprinting of (a) federal regulations about IEPs, and (b) Appendix A (formerly Appendix C) to the IDEA 97, which is a series of questions and answers about federal regulations on the IEP.

72 Point IEP Checklist http://www.isn.net/~jypsy/72iep.htm
This is a checklist of IEP related issues that the California Department of Education did recently for the schools. It is almost all federally related, and includes the relevant federal websites.

Special Education Resources on the Internet www.hood.edu/seri/serihome.htm

MODULE ONE Connecting to the Web:

The National Information Center for Children and Youth with Disabilities. This page follows a student through the process of evaluation and IEP development.
http://nichcy.org/pubs/basicpar/bpltext.htm

Federal Resource Center for Special Education. The FRC supports a nationwide technical assistance network to respond to the needs of students with disabilities, especially students from under-represented populations, follow the link to Technical Assistance. http://www.dssc.org/frc

Wrightslaw is the website of Pete Wright, an attorney whose practice is devoted to helping children with special education needs. Follow this link to information about IEPs. http://www.wrightslaw.com/advoc/articles/iep_guidance.html

The Walter Reed Army Medical Center. The Army Medical Center has a handbook for parents. This link leads to Chapter Four: Parent Role in the Educational Process.
http://www.wramc.amedd.army.mil/departments/pediatrics/efmp/handbook/CH4.htm

LDOnline provides informative articles plus useful forms to help parents and educators make the most of the I.E.P. process.
http://www.ldonline.org/ld_indepth/iep/iep.html

Individualized Education Programs – NICHCY Briefing Paper
http://www.nichcy.org/pubs/otherpub/lg2txt.htm
This publication provides substantial guidance regarding the legal requirements for developing a student's IEP. It is a verbatim reprinting of (a) federal regulations about IEPs, and (b) Appendix A (formerly Appendix C) to the IDEA 97, which is a series of questions and answers about federal regulations on the IEP.

72 Point IEP Checklist http://www.isn.net/~jypsy/72iep.htm
This is a checklist of IEP related issues that the California Department of Education did recently for the schools. It is almost all federally related, and includes the relevant federal websites.

Special Education Resources on the Internet www.hood.edu/seri/serihome.htm

Student Learning Guide to *Video Workshop for Special Education*

Module 2: Inclusion, Collaboration, and the Least Restrictive Environment

Learning Objectives:

After completing this module, you will be able to
- Define inclusion, including the philosophy of shared responsibility for the education of all children.
- Discuss how inclusion affects all students.
- Define collaboration.
- List the benefits of collaboration for teachers and their students.
- Discuss how teachers implement collaboration in a general education classroom.
- List the common barriers to collaboration.

Video Clip 2: Inclusion

Observation Questions:

1. How does the general classroom teacher involve her students in Lily's education? What are the benefits to the children in the general education classroom? To Lily?

Next Step:

1. What are the reasons some individuals and groups have objected to establishing mainstreaming and inclusion programs in the public schools?
   - What is your position on full-inclusion programs for students with disabilities?
   - What might be some benefits for them and their general education classmates?

2. Explain the concept of least restrictive environment.
   - Where did this term originate, and why?
   - How has special education changed since the laws that require this type of treatment were instituted?

   _____
   _____
   _____
   _____
   _____
   _____
   _____

3. Referring to your text, choose one of the Federal laws that you feel had the greatest impact on education for special needs students, and summarize it for your classmates. Give before and after the law examples to illustrate how this case has impacted special education.

   _____
   _____
   _____
   _____
   _____
   _____
   _____

Video Clip 3: The Collaborative Process

Observation Question:

1. In what ways do the students in this video benefit from having these two teachers plan the lesson together?

Next Step:

1. As a new teacher, how comfortable would you be with having another teacher in your classroom helping teach a subject?
   - What are some ways you could work with the teacher, or collaborate, to make the experience more beneficial to both you and your students?

2. Why is collaboration important to the process of inclusion?

3. Take a minute and think about all the teams you have been involved with.
    - Which of these teams worked well?
    - Which were not successful in meeting their goals?
    - What characteristics of collaboration were present in the teams that were successful?
    - What characteristics of collaboration were NOT present in the teams that were unsuccessful?

4. The speech/language therapist comes once a week to work with Suzanne in your classroom. Today she spent half-an-hour working on new vocabulary words with Suzanne. When she finished her work, she wanted to speak with your immediately, even though you were working with a reading group. She was very insistent and would not agree to speak later on the phone.
    - How should you handle this situation and remain collaborative with this professional?

MODULE TWO Connecting to the Web:

Find out more about inclusion at the website for the Council for Exceptional Children (CEC), http://www.cec.sped.org/.

The Inclusion Network is a non-profit organization whose staff and volunteers partner to promote inclusion of people with disabilities in the Greater Cincinnati community. http://www.inclusion.org/

Inclusion and Mainstreaming FAQs from the ERIC Clearinghouse on Disabilities and Gifted Education   http://ericec.org/faqs.html

Inclusion Resources from the Special Education Network
http://www.specialednet.com/inclusion.htm

Sharing Ideas About Teaching Effectively: Using Technology to Collaborate
http://www.cec.sped.org/bk/campbell.html

The Center for Effective Collaboration and Practice. This site includes links for parents, teachers, and others on topics stressing working together on behalf of these students. http://www.air.org/cecp/

Module 3: Cultural and Linguistic Diversity

Learning Objectives:

After completing this module, you will be able to
- Explain the differences between students who are bilingual and those who are speakers of English as a Second Language (ESL).
- Discuss instructional techniques teachers can use in multicultural classrooms.
- Discuss classroom management teachers can use in multicultural classrooms.
- Discuss the challenges of teaching in multicultural classrooms.
- Prepare a reading lesson for a classroom of students who are from diverse cultural backgrounds or include students who are ESL.

Video Clip 4: Teaching in Bilingual Classrooms

Observation Questions:

1. Why is teaching a child from a culture other than your own a special challenge? What if you have more than one culture represented in your classroom?

_____

_____

_____

_____

_____

_____

_____

Student Learning Guide to *Video Workshop for Special Education* p. 20

2. What techniques do the teachers in this clip demonstrate?

Next Step:

1. The debate over the efficacy of bilingual instruction has gone on for years and will most likely continue in this country. Browse the Internet for articles on both sides of this subject, and write about your views. Prepare a brief presentation for your classmates. *Connecting to the Web* is a good place to start your search.

2. Prepare a lesson for elementary students from diverse cultural backgrounds using one of the following books, and include a strategy for involving parents in the lesson. Visit the websites under *Connecting to the Web* on multicultural education to get ideas.

Ceremony in the Circle of Life, by White Deer of Autumn & Daniel San Souci
Children in China, by Michael Karhausen
Japanese Fairy Tales, by Philip Smith (Editor) & Kakuzo Fujiyama (Illustrator)
North American Indian Tales, by W. T. Larned, et al
All kinds: Who Cares About Race and Color? by Pam Adams
Annie and the Old One, by Miska Miles & Peter Parnall
Black Like Kyra, White Like Me, by Judith Vigna & Kathleen Tucker
Coat of Many Colors, by Dolly Parton & Judith Sutton

_____

_____

_____

_____

_____

_____

_____

_____

_____

_____

3. As a new teacher you are anxious to have good relationships with parents, so you have held open class days and parent/teacher meetings where you have provided activities for families. However, the same families always attend, but many of your families of color or from other cultures do not attend. How could you address this problem?

4. Go to the U.S. Census Bureau web site listed in *Connecting to the Web*.
    - Once you are there, find your state first and then your county. Note the racial/ethnic makeup of your state and then your country.
    - What is the majority ethnic group in your area?
    - What other ethnic groups are represented in your area?
    - How do the various ethnic groups impact your school system?

MODULE THREE Connecting to the Web:

U.S. Census Bureau: State & County Quick Facts provides access to facts from the 2000 census about people, business, and geography
http://quickfacts.census.gov/qfd/index.html

A Professor Emeritus in the Department of Secondary Education at California State University, Northridge has build a website for preparing teachers to work in ESL and bilingual classrooms includes links to lesson plans and resources that should prove valuable in the classroom.
http://www.csun.edu/~hcedu013/eslindex.html

The National Association of Bilingual Education: This organization is concerned with the quality of education received by students whose native language is not English. http://www.nabe.org

Multicultural education information is available at the Curry School of Education site. http://curry.edschool.virginia.edu/go/multicultural/teachers.html

National Association for Multicultural Education was founded in 1990 to support efforts in educational equity and social justice. http://www.nameorg.org/

Clearinghouse for Multicultural/Bilingual Education:
http://www.weber.edu/mbe/htmls/mbe.html

Student Learning Guide to *Video Workshop for Special Education*

Module 4: Learning Disabilities and Attention Deficit Hyperactivity Disorder

Learning Objectives:

After completing this module, you will be able to
- explain the characteristics of the three categories of ADHD.
- discuss the educational implications of ADHD.
- discuss the effects of ADHD on social development and personal relationships.
- debate the issues surrounding the use of medication for treatment of ADHD.
- characterize learning disabilities as noted in I.D.E.A.- '97
- provide examples of problems experienced by students with the specific type of LD known as dyslexia.
- discuss the implications of people's perceptions on the lives of children with learning disabilities.
- list instructional interventions or strategies for students with dyslexia.

Video Clip 5: ADHD

Observation Questions:

1. What characteristics of ADHD does Eric demonstrate?

_____

_____

_____

_____

_____

_____

2. Based on what you have learned about Eric, do you believe he should be included in a regular education classroom? Explain.

3. What resources should the classroom teacher pursue to help Eric succeed?

Next Step:

1. What biological causes have been determined for ADHD?

Module 4: Learning Disabilities and Attention Deficit Hyperactivity Disorder

Learning Objectives:

After completing this module, you will be able to
- explain the characteristics of the three categories of ADHD.
- discuss the educational implications of ADHD.
- discuss the effects of ADHD on social development and personal relationships.
- debate the issues surrounding the use of medication for treatment of ADHD.
- characterize learning disabilities as noted in I.D.E.A.- '97
- provide examples of problems experienced by students with the specific type of LD known as dyslexia.
- discuss the implications of people's perceptions on the lives of children with learning disabilities.
- list instructional interventions or strategies for students with dyslexia.

Video Clip 5: ADHD

Observation Questions:

1. What characteristics of ADHD does Eric demonstrate?

_____
_____
_____
_____
_____
_____

2. Based on what you have learned about Eric, do you believe he should be included in a regular education classroom? Explain.

3. What resources should the classroom teacher pursue to help Eric succeed?

Next Step:

1. What biological causes have been determined for ADHD?

2. Many people oppose the use of drugs like Ritalin to control the behaviors associated with ADHD. Others feel they are simply prescribed too frequently, and before other measures have been taken to deal with the problem.
   - Browse the Internet for issues and information from both sides of the discussion. Summarize your findings.
   - What is your opinion on the use of prescription medications with young children? With adults?

3. At the web site http://www.cdc.gov/ncbddd/adhd/dadabbur.htm you will find articles discussing the effects of ADHD on the individual's life.
    - After you read these articles, make a list of the effects you consider most important to your work as a teacher.
    - Write a brief rationale for your choices.

Video Clip 6: Learning Disabilities

Observation Questions:

1. What problems does Bridget exhibit that are symptoms of dyslexia? What concerns does she have about the effect dyslexia will have on her future?

___

Next Step:

1. Choose a common learning disability and write a brief summary of the topic to present the class. You may use your textbook or one of the websites listed in *Connecting to the Web* as a starting point.

___

2. Go to this link on the PBS special about children with learning disabilities. http://www.pbs.org/wgbh/misunderstoodminds/
   - On the left side of the main frame you will find links to Attention, Reading, Writing, and Mathematics. Follow these links to simulation activities.
   - Click on at least one of these on each page.
   - Discuss what you learned from trying the simulation.

3. Many students with learning disabilities have difficulty making and maintaining friendships.
   - What characteristics of learning disabilities contribute to this problem?
   - How do each of the characteristics you named cause problems with interpersonal relationships?

4. Use your textbook and web sites listed in the *Connecting to the Web* section to make a list of instructional interventions recommended for students with dyslexia.

MODULE FOUR Connecting to the Web:

For more information on ADHD and Ritalin, refer to the Mayo Clinic site: http://www.mayoclinic.com/invoke.cfm?id=DS00275.

National Attention Deficit Disorder Association: NADDA's mission is to help people with ADD lead happier, more successful lives through education, research, and public advocacy. http://www.add.org/

CHADD is a nonprofit parent-based organization formed to better the lives of individuals with attention deficit disorders and those who care for them. http://www.chadd.org/

National Center on Birth Defects and Developmental Disabilities has a comprehensive site about ADHD. http://www.cdc.gov/ncbddd/adhd/

International Dyslexia Association: Learn more about dyslexia or find information about membership, conferences, technology, and research. Explore the kids only site, online bookstore and message boards. http://www.interdys.org

Bright Solutions for Dyslexia: Friendly and thorough resource goes into detail about dyslexia. Check the newsletter and find out about workshops. http://www.dys-add.com/

CEC is an international, professional association with over 52,000 educator members. Their principal purpose is to advance the education of all exceptional children and youth - those with disabilities and those who are gifted. DLD is the division of the CEC that focuses on the special needs of individuals with learning disabilities. http://www.dldcec.org

The Council for Learning Disabilities (CLD) is an international organization concerned about issues related to students with learning disabilities. http://www.cldinternational.org

Schwab Learning Organization: A non-profit organization that conducts independent research and provides information about learning disabilities. http://www.schwablearning.org

Learning Disabilities Association: Advances the education and welfare of people with perceptual, conceptual, or coordinative handicaps. Factsheets, publications, and events. http://www.ldanatl.org/

LDOnline: Resource for parents, teachers and students who want to know more about learning disabilities. Includes bulletin boards and support groups. http://www.ldonline.org/

National Center for Learning Disabilities: Devoted to improving the lives of those with learning disabilities. Provides legal information and links to book lists and government agencies. http://www.ncld.org/

Module 5: Mental Retardation

Learning Objectives:

After completing this module, you will be able to
- explain the characteristics of the mental retardation as noted in I.D.E.A.-'97.
- define the classifications of mental retardation
- discuss the educational implications of mental retardation.
- discuss the effects of mental retardation on social development and personal relationships.
- explain the education program options available for students with mental retardation.

Video Clip 7: Mental Retardation

Observation Questions:

1. On which skills did the pre-school teacher focus with Carlyn?

_____

_____

_____

_____

_____

_____

_____

2. What does Carlyn gain by being included with higher functioning children?

Next Step:

1. Based on what you know from this video, in which adaptive skills is Carlyn likely to have deficits in the future? Justify your answer.

2. Using Carlyn's physical characteristics as determinants, rate the severity of Carlyn's mental retardation as moderate, severe, or profound? Justify your answer.

3. The topic of inclusion of students with mental retardation is often a controversial one.
    - Select a partner from your class to brainstorm the benefits and challenges of teaching a class that includes a student with MR.
    - Be sure to discuss all factors, not just the disability, including the student's behavior, family support, reactions of other students and their families, and special education support services.
    - Once you have generated a list, write a <u>personal reflection</u> discussing your position regarding inclusion of students with MR in general education classrooms.

4. Effective teachers of students with mild mental retardation design instructional and practice activities so that the activities relate to functional use in everyday life, including home and community.
    - Describe two instructional activities that integrate functional skills into each of these curriculum areas:
      a. reading,
      b. mathematics,
      c. writing, and
      d. listening.

MODULE FIVE Connecting to the Web:

Down's City. This site includes resources, news, and information about this syndrome. http://www.nads.org

CliniWeb International. This web site provides information about the various types of mental retardation. http://www.ohsu.edu/cliniweb/C10/C10.496.html

This is a fact sheet on mental retardation from AAMR. http://161.58.153.187/Policies/faq_mental_retardation.shtml

The Arc – a national organization on mental retardation. Includes local chapter links and information on projects, services, and education. http://thearc.org/index.htm

Student Learning Guide to *Video Workshop for Special Education* p. 41

Module 6: Communication Disorders: Language and Speech Impairments

Learning Objectives:

After completing this module, you will be able to
- summarize the role of the speech /language pathologist in the IEP process.
- explain the difference between speech and language disorders based on the definitions from I.D.E.A.-'97.
- define and give examples of the three types of speech disorders.
- describe accommodations for students with communication disorders.
- list characteristics of the two classifications of language disorders, expressive and receptive.
- discuss the effects of communication disorders on social development and personal relationships.

Video Clip 1: Individualized Education Plan

Observation Questions:

1. What speech or language deficits does Douglas demonstrate?

_____
_____
_____
_____
_____
_____
_____

2. Why does the speech pathologist feel Douglas's speech problems warrant intervention?

Next Step:

1. What is the difference between speech and language disorders?

2. What qualifications and education must a person have to be a licensed speech/language pathologist?
   - In addition to working in the schools, what career options are available?

3. Why do you think speech/language evaluation is routinely a part of an IEP meeting?
    - Of the disabilities you have studied so far in this course, which are most likely to have accompanying speech and/or language disorders?
    - How do communication disorders interfere with acquiring knowledge in school settings?

4. You have referred Juan, a native Spanish speaker, for a possible language disorder. What procedures should the speech/language pathologist follow to insure that the language disorder is appropriately diagnosed?

5. How can speech and/or language disorders affect social development and personal relationships? If the disorder does not interfere with a student's ability to learn new content, why should the school system take corrective action?

MODULE SIX Connecting to the Web:

American Speech, Language and Hearing Association www.asha.org

SERI Hearing Impairment Resources http://www.seriweb.com/hearing.htm

Speech Disorders and Teens
http://kidshealth.org/teen/health_problems/diseases/speechdisordersprt.htm

National Institute on Deafness and Other Communication Disorders is part of the National Institutes of Health. At the website noted here you can find information about communication disorders. http://www.nidcd.nih.gov/health/vsl.htm

National Center for Stuttering provides up-to-date factual information about stuttering. http://www.stuttering.com/

Module 7: Sensory Disorders: Visual and Hearing Impairments

Learning Objectives:

After completing this module, you will be able to
- Define visual impairments as noted in I.D.E.A.-'97.
- Describe the implications of a visual impairment on educational progress.
- Discuss the effects of visual impairments on social development and personal relationships.
- Define hearing impairments as noted in I.D.E.A.-'97.
- Describe the implications of a hearing impairment on educational progress.
- Discuss the effects of hearing impairments on social development and personal relationships.

Video Clip 8: Visual Impairment

Observation Questions:

1. What are some ways that Kyle compensates for his visual impairment?

_____
_____
_____
_____
_____

2. What special accommodations do his family and teacher make to enable him to function in society?

Next Step:

1. What kinds of learning difficulties would you expect from someone with a visual impairment? What accommodations might a regular classroom teacher make to enable this student to succeed in the classroom?

2. What kinds of equipment are available for visually impaired students, and how do these devices work? You should begin with a visit the website for the American Printing House for the Blind (see *Connecting to the Web*).

3. Teaching activities of daily living and orientation and mobility skills are content areas that are especially important for students with visual impairments.
   - Explain why these are important.
   - Explain why social skills will be one of the necessary activities of daily living.
   - How can these content areas be integrated into the routine teaching activities in your classroom?

Video Clip 9: Hearing Impairment

Observation Questions:

1. What special accommodations does this student require in the classroom?

2. The aide refers to the need for the teacher to use more visual teaching techniques. What kinds of things might she be referring to?

Next Step:

1. Experience what it is like to have a hearing loss by wearing earplugs to class one day and sitting in the back of the room. What does your instructor do that hinders your understanding of the content taught? What is done to aid comprehension? How might your instructor modify his or her teaching to accommodate having a hearing-impaired student in the class? Check to see what your school offers in the way of help for students with hearing deficits: sign language interpreters, closed caption video, amplifiers, etc.

2. The student in this video has partial hearing and her speech is understandable. Search the Internet for articles on the oral approach versus sign language. What do you think is the best method of communication for a child, and why? See web sites in *Connecting to the Web* for additional information.

3. Discuss the instructional implications of teaching content, beyond reading and language arts, and classroom management for general education teachers who are teaching students who are deaf or hard of hearing. Suggest an accommodation, adaptation or modification that would help meet each of these implications.

4. Placing students who are deaf in general education classrooms for all of their school day remains controversial. Parents are often unsure which professionals have the right answers. Consider both sides of this issue, then outline a plan for helping teachers and parents sort through the issues so that they may make an appropriate decision for each student.

Student Learning Guide to *Video Workshop for Special Education*   p. 56

MODULE SEVEN Connecting to the Web:

American Council of the Blind: http://www.acb.org/

The National Federation of the Blind. Founded in 1940 this consumer and advocacy organization is the nation's membership organization of blind persons with fifty thousand members. The NFB has affiliates in all fifty states plus Washington D.C. and Puerto Rico, and over seven hundred local chapters. As a, the NFB is considered the leading force in the blindness field today. http://www.nfb.org

American Printing House for the Blind: Provides texts and other educational materials in Braille and large print for students at all levels. http://www.aph.org/

The Core Curriculum for Blind and Visually Impaired Students, from Texas School for the Blind and Visually Impaired. http://www.tsbvi.edu/Education/corecurric.htm

The National Institute on Deafness and Other Communication Disorders (NIDCD) is one of the Institutes that comprise the National Institutes of Health (NIH). Established in 1988, NIDCD is mandated to conduct and support biomedical and behavioral research and research training in the normal and disordered processes of hearing, balance, smell, taste, voice, speech, and language. http://www.nidcd.nih.gov

Oral Deaf Education web site explains how new technology available today through modern hearing aids and cochlear implants provides enough access to sound that, with appropriate instruction, most deaf children can learn to talk. http://www.oraldeafed.org/

American Sign Language website provides information about the basics of signing. http://where.com/scott.net/asl/

Handspeak. Are you interested in learning about using sign language and its many uses with persons with hearing impairments, babies, and animals? Check out this site. http://www.handspeak.com

At Gallaudet University, deaf, hard of hearing, and hearing students and scholars join together in a unique community to learn, to teach, and to create. http://www.gallaudet.edu/

Student Learning Guide to *Video Workshop for Special Education*

Module 8: Emotional and Behavioral Disorders

Learning Objectives:

After completing this module, you will be able to
- Define emotional and behavior disorders as noted in I.D.E.A.-'97.
- Describe the implications of an emotional or behavior disorder on educational progress.
- Discuss the effects an emotional or behavior disorder on social development and personal relationships.

Video Clip 10: Behavior Disorders

Observation Questions:

1. What kinds of inappropriate behavior did Nick demonstrate?

2. How did the special educators at his school address these behaviors?

Next Step:

1. What qualifies a person to be designated as behaviorally disordered, as opposed to just being someone who gets in trouble for inappropriate behavior?

___

2. From what you have learned from your text and classroom discussion, what are some methods of instruction that a teacher in a regular education classroom might use with Nick?

___

3. Select a partner to complete this activity. Using information from the website in *Connecting to the Web*, prepare a PowerPoint presentation to answer the questions below. Use appropriate graphic art to illustrate your points.
   - What legal guidelines must you consider when designing discipline plans in your classroom if you have students with behavior disabilities?
   - What is a Functional Behavior Assessment? When should a teacher do the FBA?
   - What can you do to promote a positive classroom behavior?
   - What self-monitoring/self-management strategies could you use?

4. Students with behavior disorders can display two types of behavior problems: externalizing or internalizing.
   - Compare and contrast these two behaviors patterns.
   - Identify ways to manage two of these behaviors in the classroom.

MODULE EIGHT Connecting to the Web:

American Academy of Child and Adolescent Psychiatry: this site provides information is provided as a public service to aid in the understanding and treatment of the developmental, behavioral, and mental disorders that affect children and adolescents. http://www.aacap.org

The Child Psychologist: This is a private psychologist's web site that provides information about the Functional Behavior Assessment required by regulations in IDEA. http://www.childpsychology.com/fba_bip/index.htm

Kentucky State Behavior Home Page: This site provides techniques and information to help teachers and caregivers work with students who have behavior disorders. http://www.state.ky.us/agencies/behave/homepage.html

Internet Mental Health: is a virtual encyclopedia of mental health information. http://www.mentalhealth.com

Center for Effective Collaboration and Practice: This site provides resources on issues of emotional and behavioral problems in children and youth. Click on Mental Health in the left column. http://cecp.air.org/index.htm

Disruptive Behavior Disorders, from athealth.com
http://www.athealth.com/Practitioner/Newsletter/FPN_3_7.html

Behavior Disorders/Emotional Disturbance: Special Education Resources on the Internet
http://busboy.sped.ukans.edu/~music/resources/bd/bd.shtml

Emotional Disturbance Links
http://www.raevans.com/msub42.htm

SERI Behavior Disorders Resources
http://www.hood.edu/seri/behavior.htm

If you read this far, you are in for a treat: check out this page. Don't be put off by the flashing and whirling. . .this site has a wealth of information. http://maxweber.hunter.cuny.edu/pub/eres/EDSPC715_MCINTYRE/715HomePage.html

Module 9: Traumatic Brain Injury and Physical Disabilities

Learning Objectives:

After completing this module, you will be able to
- Define traumatic brain injury (TBI) as noted in I.D.E.A.-'97.
- Outline the behavior issues commonly associated with students who have TBI.
- Define physical disabilities as noted in I.D.E.A.-'97.
- Summarize the educational challenges for students who have physical disabilities.
- Discuss the effects of physical disabilities on social development and personal relationships.

Video Clip 11: Traumatic Brain Injury

Observation Question:

1. What disabilities does Matt have as a result of the TBI?

2. What skills are his teachers focusing on to enable him to eventually be included in a regular education classroom?

Next Step:

1. Prepare an argument supporting a law requiring the use of seat belts in cars and helmets when riding a bicycle or motorcycle. Cite statistics to back up your argument. Include a program for the schools to educate young children and their parents.

Student Learning Guide to *Video Workshop for Special Education*

Video Clip 12: Physical Disabilities

Observation Questions:

1. What special adaptations are made for Oscar to be able to participate in the math lesson?

_____

_____

_____

_____

_____

Next Step:

1. Use a wheelchair or any other prosthetic device for at least 3-4 hours while conducting your daily routine.
   - Did you find that your interactions with others were different in any way? What else was different?
   - What did you learn through your simulation of a physical disability?
   - How might this information help you as a teacher of a physically disabled student?

_____

_____

_____

_____

_____

2. Choose one of the organizations listed under *Connecting to the Web* and summarize what the group is doing to help people with that particular physical disability.

Student Learning Guide to *Video Workshop for Special Education* p. 67

3. Assistive technology is critically important for students with physical disabilities. Select and describe the purpose for a hardware appliance, software program, or adaptation for the following students.
    a. Student with paraplegia
    b. Student with limited use of hands and arms
    c. Student who is nonverbal.

You will find help for this activity in your text and at the following web sites:
- Closing the Gap www.closingthegap.com/
- Alphasmart is an inexpensive, personal word processing device. http://www.alphasmart.com/
- *Encarta* offers a talking dictionary. Type in a word into the "Find a word" space and follow the links. http://dictionary.msn.com/
- Alex Catalog is located at Oxford University. http://www.infomotions.com/alex/
- Web Copier allows persons to copy websites for off line use. http://www.maximumsoft.com/
- Web and/or screen readers: These are software packages that allow persons to read computer screens and web sites.
- Kurzweil. http://www.lhs.com/education/
- Web Talkster http://www.code-it.com/webtalkster.htm

MODULE NINE Connecting to the Web:

Autism Society of American, Inc. www.autism-society.org/

Association of Birth Deficit Children, Inc. www.birthdefects.org/main.htm

Brain Injury Association, Inc. www.biausa.org/

Epilepsy Foundation www.efa.org/

Families of Spinal Muscular Atrophy http://www.fsma.org/

March of Dimes Birth Defects Foundation www.modimes.org/

Muscular Dystrophy Association www.mdausa.org/

National Cystic Fibrosis Foundation www.cff.org/

National Spinal Cord Injury Association http://users.erols.com/nscia/

United Cerebral Palsy Association www.ucpa.org/

Student Learning Guide to *Video Workshop for Special Education*

Module 10: Working with Parents and Families

Learning Objectives:

After completing this module, you will be able to
- Outline the teacher's responsibilities in working with families of students with special needs.
- Identify the factors that influence the involvement of families with children with disabilities.
- Identify ways for educational professionals to work effectively with families to educate students with special needs.
- Summarize the benefits of family involvement in the education of a special needs student.
- Describe ways that families can advocate for their child with a special need.

Video Clip 13: Working with Parents and Families

Observation Questions:

1. Why should parents be actively involved in their child's education?

_____
_____
_____
_____
_____
_____
_____

2. Why might some teachers be apprehensive about having parents in the classroom?

3. What can a teacher do to involve parents?

Next Step:

1. Interview the parent of a child with a disability. Ask the parent to fill out a log for one week prior to the interview that indicates all the activities in which he or she participated with the child.
    - Was this parent actively involved in the educational process? In what ways?
    - If not, why not?
    - What conclusions can you draw from this activity?

2. Often educators fail to understand the effects that a sibling with disabilities can have on the other children in the family and therefore affect family life. Visit the web sites listed in *Connecting to the Web* under <u>Issues for Siblings.</u> Identify and list the issues faced by siblings or ways that siblings respond to the person with a disability. What is your response to these issues? How can educators help families deal with these issues?

3. In Module One of this student guide, you worked with a group to construct a handbook telling about the IEP process. Now you should join with others to write another section for that handbook. In this new section you will discuss ways that families can collaborate with professionals in schools and the community to participate in their child's education. Use the lines below to brainstorm ideas for the contents of that section. Share these with others as you begin the collaborative work on this section of the handbook.

Student Learning Guide to *Video Workshop for Special Education*

MODULE TEN Connecting to the Web:

Family Village: www.familyvillage.wisc.edu/index.html

Issues for siblings
- http://www.familyvillage.wisc.edu/general/frc_sibl.htm
- http://www.state.il.us/agency/ipcdd/council/sibling.htm
- http://www.nas.com/downsyn/siblings.html

Internet Special Education Resources (ISER): www.iser.com/

PACER Center: www.pacer.org/

Parent Pals: www.parentpals.com/

Parents Helping Parents: www.php.com/

Publication for Parents: www.ed.gov/pubs/parents/

Special Child Magazine: www.specialchild.com/

Technical Assistance Alliance for Parent Programs: www.taalliance.org/

Zero to Three: www.zerotothree.org/